INDIGENOUS HISTORY FROM 1887–1932

THE ALLOTMENT AND ASSIMILATION ERA

by E. A. Hale

FOCUS READERS®
NAVIGATOR

WWW.FOCUSREADERS.COM

Copyright © 2025 by Focus Readers®, Mendota Heights, MN 55120. All rights reserved. No part of this book may be reproduced or utilized in any form or by any means without written permission from the publisher.

Focus Readers is distributed by North Star Editions:
sales@northstareditions.com | 888-417-0195

Produced for Focus Readers by Red Line Editorial.

Content Consultant: Katrina Phillips, PhD, Red Cliff Band of Lake Superior Ojibwe, Associate Professor of History, Macalester College

Photographs ©: National Archives, cover, 1; Bettmann/Getty Images, 4–5; T. J. Morgan/Library of Congress, 7; AP Images, 9; Edward S. Curtis/Library of Congress, 10–11; C. H. Dana/Library of Congress, 13; MPI/Archive Photos/Getty Images, 14; Benedicte Wrensted/National Archives, 16–17; H. Armstrong Roberts/ClassicStock/Archive Photos/Getty Images, 18; Rodger Mallison/MCT/Newscom, 21; George Rinhart/Corbis Historical/Getty Images, 22–23; Sue Ogrocki/AP Images, 25; Red Lake News/Minnesota Historical Society/Library of Congress, 27; Carol M. Highsmith/Library of Congress, 29

Library of Congress Cataloging-in-Publication Data
Library of Congress Cataloging-in-Publication Data is available on the Library of Congress website.

ISBN
979-8-88998-412-2 (hardcover)
979-8-88998-440-5 (paperback)
979-8-88998-492-4 (ebook pdf)
979-8-88998-468-9 (hosted ebook)

Printed in the United States of America
Mankato, MN
012025

ABOUT THE TERMINOLOGY
The terms **American Indians** and **Native Americans** are used interchangeably throughout this book. With more than 570 federally recognized tribes or nations in the United States, the usage will vary. Native nations and their people may use either term. The term **Indigenous peoples** describes groups of people who have lived in an area since prehistory. It may also be used as a shorter term to describe the federal designation **American Indians, Alaska Natives, and Native Hawaiians**.

ABOUT THE AUTHOR
E. A. Hale is a proud member of the Choctaw Nation of Oklahoma.

TABLE OF CONTENTS

CHAPTER 1
Dawes Act of 1887 5

CHAPTER 2
Allotments and Curtis Act of 1898 11

CHAPTER 3
Assimilation 17

CHAPTER 4
Native Education 23

VOICES FROM THE PAST
Minnie Tsait-Kopeta 28

Focus Questions • 30
Glossary • 31
To Learn More • 32
Index • 32

CHAPTER 1

DAWES ACT OF 1887

The US Congress passed the General Allotment Act in 1887. It was also called the Dawes Act. This law affected most **Indigenous** lands. Previously, tribes owned these lands **communally**. But the new law broke **reservations** into many smaller pieces. It gave away lands that the US government had previously set

> Zitkala-Sa was a Yankton Sioux artist and activist. Her writing brought attention to the harm done by allotment.

aside for Native nations. The law tried to destroy Native **sovereignty**. But it did not.

Each tribal member got a piece of land. It was called an allotment. The Dawes Act said how Indigenous people should use the land. It said they should use it for farming or raising cattle. But some land was not good for farming or ranching. Also, many Indigenous people had been hunters and gatherers. They wanted to keep their ways of life.

The Dawes Act was also hard to follow. It said Native Americans must work each allotment for 25 years. They could not sell the land. After 25 years, the United States would give them the

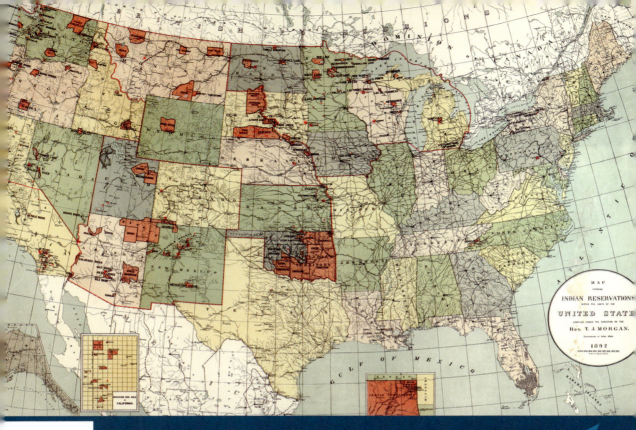

A US map from 1892 shows the locations of reservations in orange.

land. However, many American Indians lost their allotments. Some allotment owners did not read English. They did not understand allotment laws. Also, if the owner died, the land could be sold to non-Native people.

Many US settlers wanted farmland. So, the Dawes Act didn't allot all reservation land. It set aside some land to the US government. This land was called surplus land. The United States sold surplus land to settlers. Settlers did not have to wait 25 years to own it.

LAND RUNS

Dozens of tribal nations lived in the western part of future Oklahoma. This land had been promised to them through treaties. But the United States kept some of this land. Non-Native people wanted it. So, the United States set up land runs. The first was on April 22, 1889. People from many states rushed in to claim unassigned land. By 1907, US settlers owned most surplus and tribal land in western Oklahoma.

US settlers race on horseback to claim land during the first land run in April 1889.

The Dawes Act also promised US citizenship to American Indians. But they would have to give up their tribal identities. They would have to give up their **cultures**, their languages, and their ways of life.

9

CHAPTER 2

ALLOTMENTS AND CURTIS ACT OF 1898

Before allotment, Native people hunted, fished, and gathered food together. They shared food with their families and **clans**. They helped one another. However, the US government did not want American Indians to rely on their clans or tribes. It wanted each family to take care of itself.

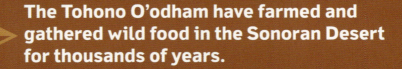

The Tohono O'odham have farmed and gathered wild food in the Sonoran Desert for thousands of years.

The Dawes Act did not apply to the **Five Tribes** in **Indian Territory**. But Congress wanted allotments there, too. So, the United States set up the Dawes Commission in 1893. The Dawes commissioners met with the Five Tribes. The team tried to get the tribes to agree to allotment. The tribes refused. They did not want their reservations broken up.

In 1896, the US government tried a new way. It wanted up-to-date tribal membership rolls. That way, it could allot land to those members when it broke up reservations. The Dawes Commission asked for old tribal rolls. It also tried to add new names to the rolls itself. The

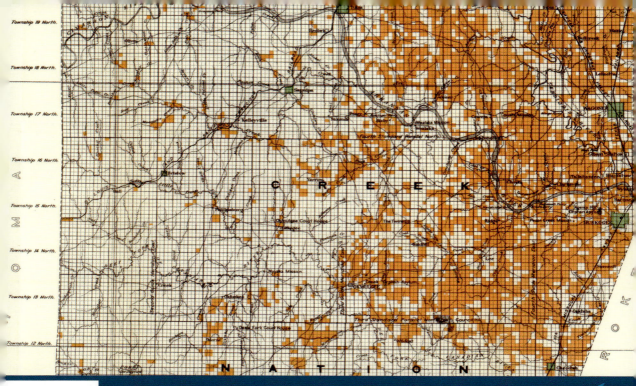

An 1899 map tracks US allotment in part of Muscogee (Creek) Nation. Each orange square shows an allotment.

Five Tribes said this went against their sovereignty. It was their right to decide who their citizens were. They did not want the US government to interfere.

The US government passed the Curtis Act in 1898. It called for a census of members in the Five Tribes. A census was

A poster from 1911 advertises the sale of Native land from allotments.

a way to get each member's name. The Five Tribes' leaders did not want this. But the act did it anyway.

Congress passed the Burke Act in 1906. It changed the Dawes Act. Native people could now sell their allotments.

But the US government also began taxing much of it. Many Native people had to sell their land to pay the taxes. By 1932, 90 million acres (36 million ha) were owned by non-Native people. Native nations lost two-thirds of the land they had in 1887.

THE CENSUS

Every 10 years, the US census counts people in the United States. Its questions change over time. In 1890, it counted all Native people as one group: American Indians. In 1900, it added Alaska Natives. It also asked for a tribal name. The 1910 census asked more questions. It asked about education. It asked the race of people's parents. The 1920 and 1930 counts asked about ethnicity and race. The census often reflects the time in which it is taken.

CHAPTER 3

ASSIMILATION

A main goal of the US government was assimilation. Assimilation meant living like most other Americans. The US government wanted Native people to give up their ways of life. This was hard for Native nations.

Many Native people wanted to live as their ancestors did. Some elders did not

> Assimilating meant dressing, speaking, and behaving differently. People risked losing their culture and identity.

Elders passed on their knowledge, cultures, and traditions to younger generations.

want to stay in one place. They wanted to be free. They recalled places to hunt and gather food.

Tribal elders had lived through US wars against Native nations. They remembered the pain of forced removals. Forced removals were when Native nations had to leave their homelands.

Elders wanted better lives for Native children. Reservation life was not healthy. Sickness hurt tribes. The children needed a safe future. So, tribes built hospitals. They built meeting houses and schools. Children learned to read and write.

Indigenous children had little knowledge of the old ways of life. For this reason, US leaders believed that they would be the easiest to assimilate. These children grew to be adults. Many of them served in the military during World War I (1914–1918). But Native

Americans often still didn't have voting rights.

Congress passed a law in 1924. It was called the Indian Citizenship Act. It made US citizens of all Indigenous people born in the United States and its territories.

CHOCTAW CODE TALKERS

Indigenous soldiers served during World War I. Some were sent to France. In October 1918, Choctaw soldiers helped send coded war messages for the United States. They talked on telephones and radios in the Choctaw language. The Germans could not break the codes. These brave soldiers were called Choctaw Code Talkers. They set the standard for a training program for future code talkers.

The Choctaw Code Talkers helped the United States win several key battles in World War I.

But state laws controlled the right to vote. A few states took until 1957 before they let Indigenous people vote.

CHAPTER 4

NATIVE EDUCATION

Indigenous people valued education. They set up schools on reservations. There were many day schools. Children went home each night after school. But some were Indian boarding schools. Students lived and studied there.

During the late 1800s, the United States set up the first of more than

> By the 1920s, about 60,000 Native children were forced into boarding schools. That was more than 80 percent of Native students.

400 **federal** boarding schools. They were overnight schools. Students slept in dormitories. Boarding schools were hard on children. Kids did not want to leave home. But children as young as six were forced to attend. These schools were often far from children's homes. Some children never saw their families again.

Students at federal boarding schools were often poorly treated. Their hair was cut off, and they wore uniforms. They were only allowed to speak English. They would be punished if they were caught speaking their own languages.

Still, US lawmakers believed Native children learned better when removed

In 2022, many Indigenous people gathered to share stories of their painful experiences at boarding schools.

from their cultures. The US government wanted to assimilate young Native Americans.

Congress passed a law in 1896. The act said taxes would no longer pay for religious schools. Taxes could pay only for federal schools. Some Native nations paid for their own religious schools closer to children's homes. Native nations believed education would help their people survive. They wanted their youth to grow up as defenders of tribal sovereignty.

Congress passed another act in 1905. This act focused on Alaska Natives. It said they could go to any Indian boarding school in Alaska. Many day schools also opened. Kids went to school near home.

Throughout all these changes, tribes kept their own knowledge. They shared information. They wrote down their own languages. With the written word, tribes kept their cultures alive. Some tribes started newspapers. Tribal elders told

Alaska, Georgia, Minnesota, Oklahoma, and South Dakota had Indigenous newspapers. Tribal newspapers were important ways to reach many Indigenous people.

stories. They sang of old ways of life. They practiced their ceremonies. They made and sold arts and crafts, such as baskets, pottery, and beadwork. Tribal sovereignty lived on.

> ## VOICES FROM THE PAST

MINNIE TSAIT-KOPETA

One federal boarding school was Carlisle Indian Industrial School in Pennsylvania. The school had strict rules. School staff punished children who broke rules. Staff wanted children to forget their cultures. Students were made to work at the school. Older students were placed in jobs. One unhappy student was Minnie Tsait-Kopeta from the Kiowa Tribe.

Minnie wrote a letter to her family in January 1913. She said she was sick. She wrote, "I shall fail in health. I am already failing." Minnie continued, "People have measles here."[1] She begged to go home to Oklahoma. Months later, Minnie had not been released from the school.

Her mother wrote to Carlisle in November 1913. She asked for Minnie to be sent home. She wrote,

Some Indigenous people are working to bring their ancestors' remains back from Carlisle's cemetery. They want all their relatives to be buried together.

"We sent her up there to school and not for work." Her mother continued, "She isn't strong and is not used to hard work."[2] Minnie finally left the school in June 1914.

Many other children got sick, too. They were too far from home. The school was too hard on them. Many died. Graves for nearly 200 children fill the Carlisle Indian School cemetery.

1. "Minnie Tsaitkopeta (Ah-Kaun) Student File." *Carlisle Indian School Digital Resource Center*. Dickinson College, n.d. Web. 5 Jan. 2024.

2. Ibid.

FOCUS QUESTIONS

Write your answers on a separate piece of paper.

1. Write a sentence explaining the main idea from Chapter 1.

2. What effect do you think boarding schools had on Indigenous children? Why?

3. Members of which Native nation were Code Talkers in World War I?
   - **A.** Kiowa
   - **B.** Muscogee (Creek)
   - **C.** Choctaw

4. Which statement shows strong Native sovereignty?
   - **A.** Native nations wrote down their own languages.
   - **B.** Native nations gave up their homelands.
   - **C.** Native nations moved to reservations.

Answer key on page 32.

GLOSSARY

clans
Extended family groups within a Native nation.

communally
Done together as a group, rather than as individuals.

cultures
The customs, arts, beliefs, and laws of groups of people.

federal
Owned or run by the top level of the US government.

Five Tribes
The Cherokee, Chickasaw, Muscogee (Creek), Choctaw, and Seminole nations who were forced to move to reservations in Indian Territory.

Indian Territory
Land reserved for forced relocation of many Native nations. The land later became eastern Oklahoma.

Indigenous
Native to a region, or belonging to ancestors who lived in a region before colonists arrived.

reservations
Land set aside by the US government for Native nations.

sovereignty
The power to make rules and decisions without being controlled by another country.

TO LEARN MORE

BOOKS

Bruegl, Heather. *Gaining US Citizenship*. Ann Arbor, MI: Cherry Lake Publishing, 2024.

Francis, Lee, III, et al. *Tales of the Mighty Code Talkers*. New York: Reycraft Books, 2020.

Stall-Meadows, Celia. *Cyrus Byington: "Sounding Horn" Missionary*. Durant, OK: Choctaw Cultural Center, 2024.

NOTE TO EDUCATORS

Visit **www.focusreaders.com** to find lesson plans, activities, links, and other resources related to this title.

INDEX

Alaska Natives, 15, 25–26
assimilation, 17, 19, 24

boarding schools, 23–24, 26, 28–29
Burke Act, 14

Carlisle Indian Industrial School, 28–29
census, 13–15

Choctaw Code Talkers, 20
Curtis Act, 13–14

Dawes Act, 5–9, 12, 14

Five Tribes, 12–14
forced removals, 17

Indian Citizenship Act, 20
Indian Territory, 8, 12

Kiowa Tribe, 28

reservations, 5, 8, 12, 19, 23

sovereignty, 6, 13, 25, 27

Tsait-Kopeta, Minnie, 28–29

World War I, 19–20

Answer Key: 1. Answers will vary; 2. Answers will vary; 3. C; 4. A